FRIENDSHIP

FRIENDSHIP

CULTIVATING THE RELATIONSHIPS THAT ENRICH OUR LIVES

Margaret Feinberg

Foreword by Marilyn Meberg

THOMAS NELSON
Since 1798

NASHVILLE DALLAS MEXICO CITY RIO DE JANEIRO BEIJING

Published in Nashville, Tennessee, by Thomas Nelson. Thomas Nelson is a trademark of Thomas Nelson, Inc.

Thomas Nelson, Inc., titles may be purchased in bulk for educational, business, fund-raising, or sales promotional use. For information, please e-mail SpecialMarkets@ThomasNelson.com.

ISBN: 978-1-4185-3414-1

Printed in China

09 10 11 12 MT 5 4 3 2 1

Contents

Contents

Foreword

As a child I used to worry about Oliver Twist. He lived in a cold, drafty orphanage in London and had to beg for more than one bowl of gruel. I could not imagine the desperation required to simply eat one bowl of gruel; to actually beg for more was astonishing. Of course it was the only food he got, so the thin, watery "porridge" was better than nothing.

I knew Oliver was a fictional character Charles Dickens thought up, but the fate of Oliver reflected the fears I had about my own future. Since I was an only child with no relatives, it would only take two bad hits to make me an Oliver.

As I think back to my early concerns for Oliver and myself, those concerns were about isolation, the fear of human disconnectedness. I never experienced that disconnectedness, but the fear of it stayed with me long past the fifth grade.

In the prison system the most dreaded form of punishment is to be put in solitary confinement. God created us for relationships, and unless one has serious anti-social tendencies, no one wants to live in "solitary." It runs counter to our God-given nature.

Scripture gives "good press" to the need and healing potential found in human relationship. Jesus traveled and ministered to others in the context of His relationship with twelve disciples. He set a great example for us to pray together, eat together, and experience the highs and lows of life together.

As you might imagine, human relatedness in the form of friendship is vital to me. One of my favorite verses on friendship is found in Proverbs 27:9. *The Message* translates it: "Just as lotions and fragrance give sensual delight, a sweet friendship refreshes the soul." A friend refreshes my soul in many ways, but my top three "refresher requirements" are humor, reciprocity (I talk, you talk, we both listen), and availability. These three refreshers contribute to my experience of connection and bonding. As I take a look at what I've just written, wouldn't those three friendship qualities make for a great discussion group?

I can just imagine you sitting with a group of women studying *Friendship: Cultivating the Relationships That Enrich Our Lives.* There's nothing as bonding as coming together as a group with the intent of learning more about each other, sharing your good times and not so good times, and laughing together over some of the crazy things that happen on life's journey.

One of my most memorable study groups included an unlikely participant by the name of Myrtle Tribunal. She was older than the rest of us, wore peculiar clothing, and spoke her mind whenever she felt like it. We were all a little unsure about how Myrtle would fit into our "format," but one of the girls in the group invited her so we went along. Myrtle soon won our hearts as she shared stories about her five children, gave advice about ours, laughed heartily about her lack of "clothes sense" and listened attentively as we shared our insecurities about marriage, careers, and relationships. She always had a wise word to say to each of us even though it was sometimes a startling solution none of us would have thought of.

One morning Myrtle simply did not wake up. We were stunned and felt the enormous loss of her presence in our lives and all that she had contributed to our group. We knew too "not waking up" would have been Myrtle's preference for leaving the earth. She never did do the expected thing.

I encourage you to use this study guide as a way of extending your borders for friendship and personal enrichment. Myrtle would assure you it's the best thing you can do for yourself.

—MARILYN MEBERG

Introduction

A Wealth of Friends

Best. Closest. Dear. Tender.
Faithful. Encouraging. Fun.

Whatever words we use to describe the friends in our lives, they can hardly contain all the joy and delight that comes from knowing and being known by someone else through the bonds of friendship.

True friends celebrate our successes and mourn our losses. They accompany us in both the unexpected and the mundane. Along the way, they remind us that in the highs and lows of life, we are not alone, and sometimes that simple realization makes all the difference.

True friends are able to speak the words that impart life, delivering a precious gift that no amount of money can buy. They have the ability to fill our hearts with hope, our spirits with encouragement, and our minds with fresh ideas and opportunities. Indeed, friends are one of the greatest gifts in life.

True friends also uncover an essential truth of life: we all need each other! Though trying to do things on your own might be enticing from time to time, there's no greater joy than sharing life and its abundant experiences with others. On a hot summer's day a fudge sundae is refreshing, but sharing it with a friend has a way of making that same ice cream taste doubly delicious.

The best kinds of friends in life are those who encourage us to be ourselves and love us despite our wrinkles and warts. They have a knack for drawing the best out of us and challenging us to grow into all we're meant to be—in our journeys of life and faith.

Now just as no two people are the same, no two friendships are the same either! They come in all different flavors. Some friends are best enjoyed over lunch at a local bistro. Other friends are meant to be celebrated over the course of a lifetime. Depending on your season in life, some friends will come and go—which is exciting because you never know when they may come around again. No matter how long or how short a person is in your life, they are worth getting to know because you never know when you might meet someone who enriches your life forever.

My hope and prayer is that through this study you'll find yourself even more grateful for all the people God has placed in your life as you continue to nurture the friendships He has given you!

Blessings,

Margaret Feinberg

Essentials
of Friendship

This first section will examine the importance of friendships and the most important friendship we'll ever have—our relationship with God. As we grow in our relationship with God, we can't help but grow in our relationship with others and learn to serve, love, and give with generosity.

One

One of Life's Greatest Gifts

As iron sharpens iron,
so one man sharpens another.

PROVERBS 27:17

Friendships were one of the original gifts from God. In the story of creation found in Genesis, when God made Adam He quickly noticed that it wasn't good for him to be alone. Then God created Eve. In addition to being the model of the first marriage, they were also best friends. God creates all of us to be in relationships and grow in our friendships.

Now it's no secret that friendships are special. Friendships are formed when we spend time with someone else. In those moments when we open up our hearts in exchanges of laughter, stories, and perspectives, we have the opportunity to grow close and form time-less bonds.

Friendships are one of life's greatest gifts. They're like treasures—you never know what you're going to discover about yourself or someone else. While friendships can bring us joy and comfort, they also contribute to our overall health and well-being. In fact, a recent study among women found that just spending time with friends can help reduce stress and produce a calming effect. If that wasn't enough, one study found that having friends can contribute not only to a happier life but also to a longer life. Not having friends or people you can really talk to has been considered as detrimental to a person's health as smoking!

> *Friendships are like treasures—you never know what you're going to discover about yourself or someone else.*

Despite all the great benefits and delights of friendships, it's easy to find ourselves too busy to nurture strong relationships. The demands of family, work, and daily chores can choke out the free time needed to maintain and grow friendships. That's why it's so important to be intentional about our friendships.

Simple activities like sending an e-mail, picking up the phone, or dropping a note in the mail can go a long way to strengthening a friendship and putting a smile on someone's face. Through small acts of kindness, we can nurture each other. We can both be a source of strength for someone else and also be strengthened. And we can grow into all God created us to be!

1. *When was the last time you had a friend who did something that saved your bad day? How did the experience make you feel? Describe it in the space below.*

2. When was the last time you had the opportunity to help save someone else's bad day? How did the experience make you feel? Describe in the space below.

3. What everyday activities have you found to be most helpful when it comes to growing and nurturing friendships?

One of the many beauties of friendship is that you don't have to face the challenges of life alone. God places all kinds of people in our lives to accompany us through the various stages of life. These relationships not only enrich our experiences but they also strengthen us.

4. Read *Ecclesiastes 4:9–10*. Can you think of a time when you specifically found this passage to be true in your own life? Explain in the space below.

One of the most important aspects of friendship is both knowing and being known. In friendship, we have the opportunity to be ourselves and allow others to really get to know us as we are. As a friendship grows deeper, we may find that the person that we're getting to know is much different than we are, but that's a good thing! Differences allow us to learn things about ourselves that we couldn't learn any other way.

When Jesus delivered the Sermon on the Mount, He spoke to a wide audience of ages, interests, and experiences. Yet He challenged each person to not judge others on a surface level but to look deeper at the issues of the heart. Jesus found hidden treasures in all kinds of people.

5. Read *Matthew 5:3–12*. Fill in each of the descriptions of those Jesus blesses with the promises that they will receive.

Blessed are the . . .	What is their reward?
Poor in spirit	(example) The kingdom of God
Those who mourn	
The meek	
Those who hunger and thirst for righteousness	
The merciful	
The pure in heart	
The peacemakers	
Those who are persecuted because of righteousness	
The insulted	

According to this passage, God blesses those who make the world a better place and treat others well. Now, it's interesting to note that none of the blessings of God, also known as the Beatitudes, can happen apart from relationships.

6. *Reflecting on the relationships in your own life, what have some of your friends taught you about God through their actions, attitudes, and involvement in your life?*

Through friendship, God gives us the opportunity to reflect His characteristics and His qualities to those around us. In friendships, we get to put into practice what we really believe about God.

7. *Think of a few of your friendships. How have they given you the opportunity to put into practice what you really believe about God?*

8. *Make a list of three friends in the space below. What specifically can you do this week to bless and encourage them?*

> *One of God's greatest gifts is friendship. God designed us to be in relationship with one another—growing, nurturing, and encouraging each other. When we're intentional about our relationships, it's amazing what God can do in and through us.*

Digging Deeper

God desires a relationship with us. As we grow to know Him, we discover more about God and His ways. Read *Psalm 119:11*. Why do you think it's so important to spend time in the Bible? How does spending time in Scripture affect your relationship with God? What happens when you go long periods of time without spending time in Scripture? How does it affect your life? Your outlook? Your relationship with God?

Ponder and Pray

The opening scripture for this lesson comes from *Proverbs 27:17*, "As iron sharpens iron, so one man sharpens another." How have you found this to be true in your life? Who would you list as some of your "iron" friends? Why do you think it's so important to build your relationship with "iron" friends?

Bonus Activity

Choose one friend to meet with on a weekly basis simply to encourage and pray for each other. Whether you connect via e-mail, phone, or in person, be intentional about your relationship and look for opportunities to connect with God together.

Two

Discovering God as a Best Friend

"I will not leave you as orphans;
I will come to you."

JOHN 14:18

One of Mary Stevenson's most popular poems is called "Footprints in the Sand," and it's been translated into many languages and treasured by millions of fans. In this poem, Stevenson depicts a dream she had where the Lord explained His role in her life. She looked out and saw her life as a journey as displayed by footprints on a sandy beach.

During the high points of life, she noticed two sets of footprints, but during the more difficult and challenging times, she only noted one set. She felt frustrated and disappointed. Where had God been? Why did He leave her all alone? Her feelings of anger budded into a sense of betrayal.

When she raised the issue to God in prayer, the Lord faithfully revealed to her that He had never left her. Those moments when she only saw one set of footprints, He had steadily been carrying her through.

At times, all of us will find ourselves asking, "Where has God gone?" and "Why do I feel all alone?" Though we may feel like God is a million miles away, the truth is that He has faithfully promised to never leave us nor forsake us. He carries us through the darkest of valleys and renews us in surprising ways when we least expect it.

Of all the relationships in our lives, our relationship with God is the most important.

Of all the relationships in our lives, our relationship with God is the most important. God wants to be our best friend—the first One we turn to in good times and bad. He wants to be our rock, our steadying hand, the One who carries us through. God wants to be our BFF—our best friend forever—and the invitation to that relationship is something that is available to us today and every day.

1. *Reflecting on the image of the woman on the beach, what are some specific times in life when you felt like you've had the pleasure of being God's friend and walking beside Him on the beach?*

2. *Reflecting on the image of the woman on the beach, what are some specific times in life when you felt as if you were all alone and God was a million miles away?*

3. *Reflecting on those moments when you felt alone in the past, can you now recognize that God was with you every step of the way? Why or why not?*

Though we may be tempted to think that God has left us on our own, Scripture reminds us that God is faithful. He is true to His word.

4. *Read **Isaiah 54:10**. What does this passage reveal about the faithfulness of God?*

5. Read *John 15:15*. How do you feel about being called a friend of God? In what way do feel like you treat God as a close friend? In what ways do you feel like you do not? Explain in the space below.

The busyness and demands of everyday life can make it challenging to connect with God and grow a relationship with Him. You may find all kinds of unexpected things getting in the way. As a result, even your best intentions to make time to connect with God may not succeed. The good news is that we have the opportunity to study the things in life that get in the way of our relationship with God and become more intentional about guarding our time.

6. Reflecting on the list below, place a check by the items that tend to distract you from spending time and nurturing your relationship with God.

____ Internet   ____ Social activities
____ Television   ____ Trying to keep up with the Joneses
____ Busyness   ____ Laziness
____ Work   ____ Other

Despite all the things that may try to distract you, God still desires a relationship with you—more than you can imagine.

7. Read **John 15:1–8**. According to this passage, what can you
   do apart from God?

8. The passage you just read in John 15 highlights the need to
   rely on God. In the space below, draw a picture of a vine and
   branches to show where you feel you are in your relationship to
   God. Add fruit to represent areas in which you feel fruitful and
   denote pruning to reveal where you feel like God is working in
   your life.

*God wants to be your best friend. He desires a
relationship with you more than you can possibly
imagine. He wants to be the first One you turn to in
good times and bad.*

Digging Deeper

Throughout His life, death, and resurrection, Jesus showed us count-less examples of His love for us. Read *John 13:3–10*. Now imagine Jesus asking to wash your feet. Would you be excited or hesitant about the experience? Why? Are there any areas of your life where you're hesitant to express dependence on God or try to do things on your own? Prayerfully take these to God.

Ponder and Pray

The opening scripture for this lesson comes from *John 14:18*: "I will not leave you as orphans; I will come to you." In what ways have you found this to be true in your own life? Why is God's faithfulness so important to your faith journey? How does knowing that God will never leave you nor forsake you make you feel?

Bonus Activity

On a blank piece of paper, make a list of seven things you consider essential in a good friend. Examples include compassion, trustwor-thiness, and honesty. Over the course of the next week, spend time searching for scriptures that identify God with one of these qualities. Ask God to reveal Himself to you in new and unexpected ways.

Three

Discovering God's Friends

They devoted themselves to the apostles'
teaching and to the fellowship, to the breaking
of bread and to prayer.

ACTS 2:42

A group of lifelong friends decided to purchase a parcel of land together in the mountains of North Carolina and build homes on the property. They had spent their lives together, and now they wanted to retire together. Each couple carefully designed their individual houses with loving care and attention to detail.

One day a visitor came to the property and visited one of the homes. The visitor couldn't help but notice the wide, beautiful doorways throughout the house.

"I really like your doorways," the visitor commented.

"Oh, those are for our neighbor," the owner answered.

"Why did you design your home for someone who doesn't even live here?"

"Because while we were building our home, our neighbor began suffering from multiple sclerosis. Within months she was using a wheelchair. Most doors come in a small standard size. For our doors to always be open to her, we need them to be thirty-six inches, which is standard for wheelchair accessibility. They're expensive but they're worth every penny because our dear friend and neighbor feels comfortable coming over and visiting whenever she wants—even when we're not here."

Loving God means loving His people, including those who don't know Him yet.

Friendship with God is not just between you and God but also extends to your relationship with others. Loving God means loving His people, including those who don't know Him yet. Just like the story of the life-long friends who built their homes so others could feel welcome, we have the opportunity to build our lives in such a way that we can welcome others. Like the doors that were built slightly wider, we can open our hearts to those who may be different than us but need to experience God's love nonetheless. And in the process, we may find ourselves being loved in ways we wouldn't experience any other way.

1. *Have you ever had someone do something significant like building custom doors to show their love and appreciation of you? If so, explain. How did it impact your life?*

2. *Have you ever done something significant like building custom doors to show your love and appreciation to someone else? If so, explain. What was the result?*

3. *Why do you think it's important to keep the door of your heart open to others?*

When Jesus was asked about the greatest commandment and how to inherit eternal life, He actually listed two commands that go hand in hand.

4. *Read **Luke 10:25–28**. Does loving God or loving your neighbor come more naturally for you? Explain.*

5. Why do you think it's so important to God that we love others?

The story in Luke doesn't end with Jesus simply explaining the two commandments. He illustrates these commands with a powerful story.

*6. Read **Luke 10:29–37**. Why do you think the temptation is to look the other way when we see someone in need?*

One of the most amazing things about the stories and parables that Jesus told is that we are invited to look at the stories from different angles and perspectives. Though we may naturally relate to one person in a story Jesus taught, it's important to carefully examine each person mentioned. Studying each person's perspective helps the story come alive, and we can learn more through it.

7. Which of the three men described in this passage best portrays your everyday attitude toward your neighbors?

8. *Are there any opportunities in your life right now where you feel God calling you to be the Good Samaritan? Explain. Is anything stopping you from getting involved?*

> *As a friend of God, you are called and created to love others. Loving others and loving God go hand in hand.*

Digging Deeper

Loving others means looking for opportunities to serve. Read *Matthew 28:20–28*. How did Jesus demonstrate what it means to be a servant through His life? Why do you think service is so important in expressing love? How do you show your love for others? Who are you serving right now?

Ponder and Pray

The opening scripture for this lesson comes from *Acts 2:42*: "They devoted themselves to the apostles' teaching and to the fellowship, to the breaking of bread and to prayer." How does spending time with other believers strengthen your faith? Why do you think it's important to be intentional about talking about spiritual issues in everyday life with fellow believers?

Bonus Activity

Look for an opportunity to show God's love to someone who is new in your community this week. Consider baking a dessert, inviting them to share a meal, or spending time serving them in a specific way. Share your story with your study group the next time you gather.

Your Friendship Circle

This section will examine twelve different types of friends you shouldn't be without! When you reflect on your relationships, you should have at least one of each type among your companions who will challenge you to become all you're called to be.

Four

Friends Who Teach Us Something

*You, however, know all about my teaching, my way
of life, my purpose, faith, patience, love, endurance.*

2 TIMOTHY 3:10

It's no secret that relationships are one of God's greatest gifts. The beauty of connecting with others is that we have the opportunity to develop friendships with people who are very different from us.

When we look at our friendship circles, it's important to include friends who can teach us new things. Through these relationships we may be exposed to new experiences and ideas. We discover a new hobby, sharpen our cooking skills, or visit a place near our home we never knew about before! In the process we learn things about ourselves, life, and God that we couldn't learn any other way.

In the Bible we read about a special relationship between Paul and Timothy. Paul was a mentor to Timothy and served as an older, wiser voice in his life. Paul encouraged the young leader as he prepared him to handle the church at Ephesus. Not only did Paul root for Timothy, but he also served as a source of wisdom and strength and a cheerleader in the faith.

But relationships aren't just one-way exchanges! Undoubtedly Timothy enriched Paul's life and faith journey as well. Through Timothy, Paul had the opportunity to pour all the wisdom and joy of life into someone else. He was able to share some of the life lessons he had learned the hard way. He shared his faith in a tangible way by investing in Timothy. Having people like Paul and Timothy—someone who mentors us as well as those we mentor—can add richness and beauty to life!

Friendships can expose us to new experiences and ideas.

Another special relationship in the Bible was between two sisters, Mary and Martha. In some ways, these sisters couldn't have been any more different from each other. Mary was known for her quiet spirit and deep love of Jesus; Martha was known for her hard work ethic, willingness to serve, and ability to get things done. Though they had moments of conflict, they learned to work through their disagreements. Whether or not you have a familial sister, you have many sisters in Christ: women who come along side of you and enrich your life's journey. They challenge you, encourage you, and help you become all you were created to be in more ways than you can imagine.

Though Paul and Timothy as well as Mary and Martha were very different from one another, they each learned from one another. In their friendships, they were both teacher and student. And that's a kind of friendship we could all benefit from!

1. When you think about people who have enriched your life simply because you know them, who comes to mind?

The relationship between Paul and Timothy is a wonderful reminder of what can happen when we invest in others as well as allow others to invest in us.

2. Read *1 Timothy 1:2* and *2 Timothy 1:2*. How does Paul describe Timothy? What does this reveal about the closeness of their friendship?

3. Why do you think it's important to have someone who mentors you as well as someone you mentor? Who has been a Paul in your life? Who has been a Timothy in your life?

4. *If you don't have a Paul or a Timothy in your life right now, what steps can you take to develop mentor/mentee relationships?*

We can learn valuable lessons from the relationship between Mary and Martha. Though these two women loved Jesus very much, their expressions of that love couldn't have been more different. As a result, we have the opportunity to learn from both of them.

5. *Read **Luke 10:38–42**. How was Mary's response to the situation different than Martha's? What does their difference in responses reveal about their personalities?*

6. *Can you think of a time when a friend's patience and listening skills helped get you through a rough time? Why is it important to have a Mary in your life?*

7. *Can you think of a time when a friend's hard work and diligence helped get you through a rough time? Why is it important to have a Martha in your life?*

8. *What steps can you take this week to show appreciation for the Marys and Marthas in your life?*

Friends can teach you all kinds of amazing lessons about life and God. Four friends to consider inviting into your life: someone who can mentor you (like Paul), someone you can mentor (like Timothy), someone who shows love through quiet listening (like Mary), and someone who shows love through service (like Martha).

Digging Deeper

Paul expressed much of his love, concern, and wisdom for leading the church in his letters to Timothy. Read either 1 *Timothy* or 2 *Timothy*. As you read, reflect on the tone, the moments of encouragement, and the wisdom Paul expressed to this young leader.

Ponder and Pray

The opening scripture for this lesson comes from *2 Timothy 3:10*: "You, however, know all about my teaching, my way of life, my purpose, faith, patience, love, endurance." Why do you think it's so important to be open and share your heart with your friends? How does going deeper in your friendships affect your faith?

Bonus Activity

Over the course of the next week, think about a Mary and a Martha in your own life. Then take time to write a letter of appreciation to both of those people—one who has taught you how to serve faithfully as well as one who has taught you how to grow in your faith through stillness.

Five

The Inner Circle of Friends

"Where are you staying?"
"Come," [Jesus] replied, "and you will see."

JOHN 1:38–39

Crowds of people followed Jesus wherever He went. At times, He probably felt like a sardine—with so many people pushing up against Him! In the Gospels, we read that Jesus prayerfully considered those who would become His closest friends. He spent time in prayer before He selected the twelve disciples—the men with whom He would embark on three years of active ministry. In the process of doing life and ministry together, they developed deep bonds. They traveled together, ministered together, and lived on the road together. Jesus' choices in disciples reveals something about the richness that comes from a diversity of friends.

Just as Jesus took time to prayerfully consider who He was supposed to spend the majority of his time with, we, too, should prayerfully ask for God's wisdom and guidance in our closest relationships.

We should also pay attention to some of the choices Jesus made in His friendships.

One of the first disciples that Jesus called was John. He had a special and close relationship with Jesus. In the Gospel of John, he describes himself as the disciple "whom Jesus loved" (John 20:2). He recognized his relationship with Christ was not just as a follower but as a friend. All of us need people in life whom we are particularly close to—people with whom we can share our most intimate dreams and desires.

Another disciple that Jesus called was Peter. Now Peter was full of energy and enthusiasm even in areas where he wasn't experienced. Though a bit impetuous, he learned from his mistakes and in the process, taught us rich lessons of faith. All of us need people in our lives who are willing to try new things, take risks, and learn from their mistakes. These friends can help us grow, expand our horizons, and become all God has created us to become.

We should prayerfully ask for God's wisdom and guidance in our closest relationships.

Some might be surprised that Jesus called Thomas to be a disciple. After all, he's known for asking some pretty tough questions! Dubbed "doubting Thomas," he wasn't afraid to ask for proof that Jesus had really come back to life. What's interesting is that Jesus didn't scold him for this request. Instead, He just showed him that He really was alive. The Thomases in our lives ask the tough questions and in the process help us grow in our faith.

One of the most intriguing disciples of Jesus was Nathanael. He was not one to mince words. When it came to honesty, Nathanael didn't hold back. He spoke what he really thought, and in the process challenges all of us to be more honest in our relationship with God.

John, Peter, Thomas, and Nathanael undoubtedly frustrated Jesus at times, but they also brought Him great delight with their unique personalities, character, and laughter. Just as all of Jesus' disciples enriched His journey, we need a circle of friends who will enrich our own.

1. *Do you think that Jesus became friends with His disciples? Why or why not?*

2. *When you think about the disciples of Jesus, with whom do you identify the most? Who do you think would be the disciple that would be the toughest for you to get along with?*

3. *Read **John 13:23**, **John 21:7**, and **John 21:20**. How did John refer to himself in these passages? Why do you think he referred to himself this way?*

4. *How do you know when you are truly loved by a friend? Who is John in your life right now?*

5. *Read **Matthew 14:22–33**. Who was the first person to respond to Jesus' appearance? What does this story reveal about Peter's personality and strengths as a friend and follower of Jesus? Who is a Peter in your life right now?*

Thomas is famous for being the "doubting disciple." He wanted to know for sure that Jesus had really risen from the dead. But that wasn't the only tough question Thomas was willing to ask.

6. *Read **John 14:1–6**. What was the tough question Thomas asked Jesus (verse 5)? How does Jesus respond (verses 6–7)? In what ways have friends who ask tough questions enriched your life? Who is a Thomas in your life right now?*

Nathanael was known for honesty. He was a man who was not willing to hold back what he really thought.

7. Read **John 1:43–50**. *How does Jesus describe Nathanael (verse 47)? Why do you think it's so important to have friends in your life who are refreshingly honest? Who is a Nathanael in your own life right now?*

8. *Who is in your inner circle of friends? How are they challenging you to grow personally and in your faith journey?*

> When Jesus selected the disciples, He did not pick people who would become His followers, but those who would become His friends. His choices in the disciples reveal something about the richness that comes from a diversity of friends as demonstrated in His relationships with John, Peter, Thomas, and Nathanael.

Digging Deeper

Philip was another disciple and friend of Jesus. Read *John 6:15*. What was Philip's response to the situation? What did this reveal about his personality? His personal strengths? Who in your life is like Philip right now?

Ponder and Pray

The opening scripture for this lesson comes from *John 1:38–39*: "'Where are you staying?' 'Come,' [Jesus] replied, 'and you will see.'" Why do you think Jesus surrounded Himself with so many different types of people? Are you as willing to surround yourself with many different types of people? Why or why not?

Bonus Activity

Make a list of your twelve closest friends. Next to each name, make a list of the person's strengths and how he or she enriches your life. Spend time in prayer thanking God for each person.

Six

Unexpected Friendships

*Religion that God our Father accepts as pure and
faultless is this: to look after orphans and widows
in their distress and to keep oneself from being
polluted by the world.*

JAMES 1:27

A friend-filled life means having people of all different backgrounds.
They may come from different nations, cultures, or backgrounds
that are far different from your own experience. And they may come
in the most unexpected ways! You never know when life is going to
take a turn and you're going to meet someone truly remarkable.

Jesus told a compelling story about a poor man named Lazarus
who sat at the gate of the city, begging. Though he did not have
material wealth, he found great favor in the eyes of God. Jesus made
it clear that we need to reflect the kindness and generosity of God
to people in a practical way. You never know when you might have
the unexpected opportunity to befriend a Lazarus, but one thing is
for sure: your life won't be the same again!

A rather unexpected friendship in the Bible was between Jesus and Joseph of Arimethea. Joseph of Arimethea displayed his love for God in a tangible way. He was a rich man, and he used his wealth to provide a place of burial for Jesus. He had no idea that his gift of a tomb would become the place where Jesus rose from the dead, but he gave freely anyway. Unlike Lazarus, Joseph of Arimethea had great wealth, but he managed to use his resources to reflect the kindness and generosity of God in a meaningful way. Sometimes we may find a person like Joseph of Arimethea offering us an unexpected gift or kindness. Or we may have the opportunity to be a Joseph of Arimethea to someone else.

Friendships may come in the most unexpected times and places, but they're always worth celebrating.

Jesus must have surprised almost everyone when He befriended Zacchaeus, a man of questionable repute. This short man climbed a sycamore tree to get a glimpse of the Son of God. Upon encountering Jesus, he agreed to give half his possessions to the poor and pay back those he had cheated four times the amount! Sometimes it's all too easy to look at people like Zacchaeus and dismiss the possibility that they'd ever want a relationship with Jesus. But in the process of friendship, we may discover that they're closer to a relationship with God than we ever imagined. Unexpected friends like Zacchaeus help us stay on our toes!

In an often-overlooked story in the Bible, we see that Paul found a very unexpected friendship in a slave named Onesimus. In the short book of Philemon, we read that Paul asks that Onesimus's owner set him free. In the process, Paul teaches us a valuable lesson about the importance of having someone to defend in your life. Do you have a friend whom God has called you to stick up for or protect? If so, you may have some incredible opportunities to put your faith into action!

God invites you to open your heart to all different friendships—with people who are poor and rich, those who are slightly misguided as well as those who are on track, and those who need someone to speak up on behalf of them. These kinds of friendships may come in the most unexpected times and places, but they're always worth celebrating.

1. *Can you think of a time when you befriended someone who was much different from you? How were you enriched from the experience? How did your faith grow?*

2. *What's your greatest challenge of befriending people who are different from you?*

Jesus highlighted the importance of reaching out to those who are different from us. One of the most compelling stories of this is that of the rich man and Lazarus. The rich man was dressed in the finest clothes and enjoyed a luxurious life. Every time he left his estate, he passed by the same beggar sitting at the gate. Lazarus was poor, hungry, and covered with sores.

> 3. Read **Luke 16:19–31**. What about this story inspires you in
>   your own faith journey?

> 4. Have you ever had a Lazarus in your life? If so, how did you
>   respond? If not, how would your own faith journey be enriched?

Sometimes the most unexpected people make the biggest impact. After the death of Jesus, we read that Joseph of Arimathea did something rather extraordinary.

5. *Read Mark 15:43–46. In what ways does Joseph of Arimathea inspire you to give generously? Can you ever really know the impact a gift might have? Why or why not?*

Another unexpected friendship arose between a sketchy guy named Zacchaeus and Jesus. As the chief tax collector, Zacchaeus was known for taking advantage of people. Yet instead of ignoring him, Jesus sought Zacchaeus out. He found the short man in a rather uncomfortable position—sitting in a sycamore tree. Jesus called out to Zacchaeus, and as a result a friendship formed that changed the tax collector's life forever.

6. *Read Luke 19:1–9. Does Zacchaeus's response to Jesus surprise you? Why or why not?*

The book of Philemon centers on a wealthy Christian and Onesimus, his runaway slave. In Rome, Onesimus meets Paul and becomes a follower of Jesus. Recognizing that Onesimus should not have run away from his slave owner, Paul sends him back. But he includes a powerful note asking the wealthy Christian to give Onesimus his freedom and recognize him not as a slave but as a brother. Paul's letter is a reminder that love and reconciliation get top billing among believers.

7. Read **Philemon**. What kind words does Paul use to describe Onesimus? Why do you think it's so important to defend those who are defenseless and give voice to those who cannot speak on their own behalf?

Take a moment and reflect on the four people discussed in this session: Lazarus, Joseph of Arimathea, Zacchaeus, and Onesimus.

8. Do you have friends who portray each of these individuals in your life? Why or why not? In what ways is God inviting you to expand your friendship circle to include others?

Great friends will come from a variety of backgrounds. Four types of friends who can enrich your life are represented by Lazarus, Joseph of Arimethea, Zacchaeus, and Onesimus.

Digging Deeper

Paul couldn't say enough great things about Onesimus. Read *Colossians 4:8*. Why do you think Paul was so concerned for Onesimus? What do you think was special about their relationship? Have you ever defended someone who couldn't defend themselves? How did this enrich your friendship and relationship with that person?

Ponder and Pray

The opening scripture for this lesson comes from *James 1:27*: "Religion that God our Father accepts as pure and faultless is this: to look after orphans and widows in their distress and to keep oneself from being polluted by the world." Why do you think it's important to befriend those in need? Who has been a friend to you when you were in need? How did it impact your life? Who is God calling you to befriend right now?

Bonus Activity

Go online and spend some time researching opportunities to care for those who are outside of your comfort zone. You may find people in your own church or community in whose lives you can make a difference. You may also discover other organizations that are making a difference around the world by committing to alleviate poverty, fight AIDS, or end human trafficking. Look for specific ways to put your faith into practice.

Hindrances to Friendship

This section will explore some of the hindrances to the friendships you were designed to enjoy. It will help you get past those hindrances to ensure that you develop the healthiest, strongest friendships possible!

Seven

Untying Knots of Jealousy

Place me like a seal over your heart, like a seal on
your arm; for love is as strong as death, its jealousy
unyielding as the grave. It burns like blazing fire,
like a mighty flame.

SONG OF SOLOMON 8:6

A young man name Clyde was an accomplished cartoonist. He had studied the art of drawing long enough to tell good work from bad, and he wasn't afraid to share his insights and opinions with those who really wanted to know what he thought. Those who were courageous enough to ask Clyde found their work improving and encouragement in their craft of drawing.

One of Clyde's friends, Norman, loved drawing. Though he had some work published, Clyde knew that Norman had immense potential. But one day Clyde noticed that Norman was particularly down on himself. Clyde went out of his way to encourage the young man.

"Why don't you do a cover and show it to the *Saturday Evening Post*?" he challenged.

Norman looked at him quizzically. But Clyde went on to make a case that Norman's work wasn't just good enough for publication, but good enough for one of the nation's best magazines. The young artist took the word of encouragement to heart. And shortly after, Norman Rockwell sold his first painting to the *Saturday Evening Post*. He went on to become one of America's most beloved artists. One encouraging word from a friend made all of the difference!

> *The encouraging words of a friend sometimes make all the difference!*

But what would have happened if Clyde would have held back his kind words? What would have happened if he would have allowed jealousy to get the best of him or his relationship with Norman Rockwell? No one knows, but what we do know is that the encouraging words of a friend sometimes make all the difference!

That's why it's important to guard your friendships from anything—like jealousy—that can undermine the relationship. Real friends challenge each other to become the very best person they can be and offer kind words on life's difficult days. True friends bring out the best in each other.

1. *Reflecting on your own life, who has been a true friend to you by being a voice of encouragement?*

2. Why is encouragement so important to a healthy relationship? To daily life?

3. Why do you think it's so important to guard your relationships from jealousy? Have you ever had jealousy short-circuit one of your friendships? Explain.

We've all experienced jealousy at one time or another, and it's never pretty. Rather than celebrating with others for what they have or have been given, jealousy invites us to turn inward and focus on what we do not have. The result is contempt for the other person. Jealously can have bad results in any relationship or friendship. This was displayed early in the book of Genesis between two brothers, Cain and Abel.

4. Read **Genesis 4:1–16**. Why was Cain angry and jealous of Abel?

5. What was God's response to Cain's anger and jealousy (verses 6–7)? What was Cain's response to God's instruction (verse 8)?

6. In what ways have you seen jealousy kill a friendship?

The good news is that jealousy does not have to get the best of a friendship! In fact, when two people choose to support, encourage, and honor each other, friendships can grow strong and deep. David and Jonathan had an amazing friendship! Though the two men could have grown jealous of each other—Jonathan was the king's son, but David had been appointed heir to the throne—they exhibited nothing but love, kindness, and support for each other.

7. Read *1 Samuel 20:1–42*. How did Jonathan show his faithfulness to David as a true friend?

8. Have you ever had a David-and-Jonathan friendship with someone? If so, describe. Why is it so important to guard those relationships from jealousy?

Jealousy can try to creep into any great friendship, but we can guard our relationships from jealousy by loving others and celebrating their successes.

Digging Deeper

Read *Proverbs 27:4*. What are some tactics you can take to guard your relationships from jealousy? What can you do to make sure you don't provoke jealousy in other people?

Ponder and Pray

The opening scripture for this lesson comes from *Song of Solomon 8:6*: "Place me like a seal over your heart, like a seal on your arm; for love is as strong as death, its jealousy unyielding as the grave. It burns like blazing fire, like a mighty flame." Once jealousy is lit within a relationship, its flames can be hard to put out. Are there any relationships in your life where you've allowed jealousy to get the best of you? What can you do to restore these relationships?

Bonus Activity

Love is a powerful force when it comes to snuffing jealousy in a relationship. Think of three friends and do something especially kind for them. Show your love in words, actions, or deeds.

Eight

Using Your Words as Balm

Words from a wise man's mouth are gracious,
but a fool is consumed by his own lips.

ECCLESIASTES 10:12

There is a wonderful story told of a family with teenage children who committed themselves to not criticize each other in any way on Sundays as part of the Sabbath celebration. The weeks rolled into months as the commitment became a healthy habit for the family. As time went by, the family noticed more and more of the teenagers' friends were coming over on Sundays just to hang out. Though no one had shared the details of the commitment, the teenage visitors knew that the home was a great place to hang out!

It's amazing what kind and encouraging words can do to bring people together. Just as a home without criticism attracts lots of friends, a home filled with criticism can keep people away. The same can be said about a friendship. Though at times we may find harsh words trying to escape our lips, we must try to capture every one. Once a harsh word is spoken, it can be like a sword,

*Intentionally
choose words
that impart
life, hope, and
encouragement.*

causing deep pain to someone else. That's why it's so important to be intentional about choosing words that impart life, hope, and encouragement.

Albert Schweitzer once said, "Sometimes our light goes out but is blown into flame by another human being. Each of us owes deepest thanks to those who have rekindled this light." The power of words is amazing! The words you choose can literally heal and give hope. That's why it is so important to choose our words wisely and season our speech with love, grace, and kindness. Great friendships are built on caring and sharing—and words go a long way to make sure those sentiments are expressed and felt.

1. *What are the most encouraging things someone has said to you recently? How did the encouragement make you feel? How did it make you want to treat others?*

2. *When was the last time someone said something discouraging to you or used words that stung? Which do you think stays with you longer—encouraging words or hurtful words? Explain.*

3. Read **James 3:6**. How have you seen this to be true in your own life?

Proverbs is a book of wisdom packed with all kinds of insights on life. Throughout Proverbs, we read constant reminders of the importance of choosing our words wisely and seasoning our speech with love, kindness, and grace. These nuggets of wisdom help protect us from not only what comes out of our mouths but also what resides in our hearts.

4. What advice do the following verses in Proverbs provide regarding your speech:

Proverbs 11:9:

Proverbs 13:3:

Proverbs 21:23:

5. In what way do you find the verses in Proverbs to be true in your own life?

6. *According to the passages below, what are some of the benefits of choosing your words wisely?*

   Proverbs 16:24:

   Isaiah 50:4:

   1 Peter 3:10:

7. *Read **Ephesians 5:19–20**. What are some practical ways you can put this passage into action in your own life?*

8. *Is there anyone with whom you have recently spoken harshly that you need to apologize to? What's stopping you from repairing the relationship?*

Words are incredibly powerful! That's one reason it's so important to choose our words wisely and season our speech with love, grace, and kindness.

Digging Deeper

Read *Proverbs 17:27*. Do you consider yourself a person of understanding? Why or why not? When is it most challenging for you to restrain your words? When it is easiest? Spend some time in prayer asking God to give you the wisdom and strength to restrain your words the next time you're tempted to say something inappropriate.

Ponder and Pray

The opening scripture for this lesson comes from *Ecclesiastes 10:12*: "Words from a wise man's mouth are gracious, but a fool is consumed by his own lips." What steps can you take to ensure your words are seasoned with grace? Are there any changes you need to make in your tone or rate of response to a situation to soften your words?

Bonus Activity

Make a commitment not to criticize anyone (including yourself!) for the next five days. Keep a journal of how this exercise affects your attitude, your faith, and your relationships.

Nine

Ensuring Selfishness
Doesn't Win

*Therefore, if anyone is in Christ, he is a new
creation; the old has gone, the new has come!*

2 CORINTHIANS 5:17

The powerful movie *Schindler's List* tells the story of a German named Oskar Schindler, who unselfishly and at great risk to himself, helped save more than a thousand Jews who were destined to Auschwitz. The film recounts Schindler's discovery of the Jewish Holocast and his ingenious plan to save as many lives as he possibly could. He discovered that he could hire Jews to work in his factory that designed military products for Germany. While the job protected them from exportation to the concentration camps, they were also directed to intentionally sabotage the ammunition being created for Germany. Though at the beginning of the war Schindler was a rich businessman, by the end of the film he was nearly bankrupt because of his efforts to save the Jewish people.

At the end of the film, Schindler meets with his workers and tells them that the war is over and they can go free. In a particularly moving scene, Schindler embraces his financial manager in tears and declares, "I could have done more." Looking around, he sees his car and asks, "Why did I save this? I could have bought ten Jews with this." Then he looks at another small item and cries out, "This could have saved another one." Oskar Schindler's willingness to sacrifice in order to save and protect others is both inspiring and compelling. His life was an example of the impact unselfish living can have on others.

> *Live generously and look for every opportunity to put others first.*

The willingness to give, serve, and sacrifice begins in our one-on-one relationships. When we choose to live unselfishly with our friends, it naturally strengthens relationships and brings people together. But living selfishly with a me-centered attitude can tear people apart. Like heavy rains on a dry plain, selfishness can erode a relationship. It has the ability to uproot love, trust, and understanding. This is one reason that it is so important to live generously and look for every opportunity to put others first. When we honor others by placing their needs above our own, there's no telling how many lives we may have the opportunity to impact.

1. Why do you think being unselfish is so important to healthy friendships?

2. *There will always be give and take in a healthy friendship. What are some ways you can ensure there's a good balance of give and take in your relationships?*

Sometimes it's hard to recognize when selfishness creeps into a situation or relationship, but the fruit is all too often conflict and heartache. One story of how selfishness almost resulted in death is found in the story of two women in the Old Testament.

3. *Read **1 Kings 3:16–28**. Which of the women was clearly selfish about the living son? How was the selfishness displayed?*

4. *In what ways was Solomon's wisdom displayed in his response to the situation?*

One of the most harmful things about selfishness is that it breeds all kinds of unbecoming behavior and attitudes. When we are focused on ourselves above all others, we allow other sins and hurtful actions to run rampant in our lives.

5. Read *James 3:14–18*. *According to this passage, what are some of the fruits of selfishness? How can these undermine your friendships?*

6. *According to this passage, how are we supposed to live?*

The good news is that through Jesus Christ we can be empowered to serve and love others. We don't have to let selfishness get the best of us. Instead, we can walk in humility, placing others before ourselves and allowing the love of God to flow through us.

7. Read *Philippians 2:3–4*. *What does this passage suggest when it comes to building healthy relationships? How have you found this passage to be true in your own life?*

8. *In what ways can maintaining an eternal perspective and a Jesus-centered focus help you uproot any selfishness in your life?*

> *Friendships are so precious! We have to protect and guard them against selfishness, which can undermine a great relationship.*

Digging Deeper

Read *Hebrews 4:12–13*. Have you ever had this passage ring true in your own life? If so, explain. In what ways can spending time in Scripture help you live more unselfishly? How can spending time reading God's Word help you live more generously and be better in tune with the needs of those around you?

Ponder and Pray

The opening scripture for this lesson comes from *2 Corinthians 5:17*: "Therefore, if anyone is in Christ, he is a new creation; the old has gone, the new has come." In what ways does becoming a Christian invite you to be less self-centered? Why do you think it's important to keep our eyes on Christ every single day? How does focusing on God make you less selfish?

Bonus Activity

Make a list of specific ways that you can put the needs of others above your own this week. What opportunities do you have to serve others? What can you do to give with abandon and truly make a difference in someone's life? Keep a journal of your experiences, and share them with your spiritual community.

Satisfying Friendships

*This final section will explore how to
develop satisfying, rewarding relationships.
It will encourage you to choose forgiveness
and unity and celebrate the wondrous
friendships God has given you!*

Ten

The Power of Forgiveness

For if you forgive men when they sin against you,
your heavenly Father will also forgive you.

MATTHEW 6:14

A story is told of Abraham Lincoln as he went down to a slave block to purchase a young slave girl. She looked with fear at the tall white man, who she assumed was just going to buy her and abuse her like the other slave owners had done. He won the bid and, now as his property, she followed him out of the slave block.

"You're free," Lincoln said.

"What does that mean?" she asked.

"It means you're free," he explained.

"Does that mean that I can say whatever I want to say?" she asked.

"Yes!" he answered.

"Does that mean that I can be whatever I want to be?" she asked.

"Yes!" he answered.

"Does that mean I can go wherever I want to go?" she asked.

"Yes!" he answered.

"Then I will go with you," she said, with tears streaming down her face.

Abraham Lincoln chose to erase or "forgive" the debt. That's what makes this story such a powerful reminder of what forgiving someone can really do. When we forgive someone—or let their debt go—then we free them to become all that they were created to be. Indeed, forgiveness may be one of the most powerful things we ever do!

When we forgive someone, we free them to become all that they were created to be.

When we choose to forgive the people and the incidents that hurt us, as well as ask for forgiveness when we hurt others, then we help ensure that no snare gets in the way of our relationships and friendships. No friendship or relationship can survive without forgiveness. Forgiveness is a powerful healer and helps ensure that our friendships truly last a lifetime.

1. *In your own life, how have you seen forgiveness restore or renew friendships?*

2. *Have you ever experienced a relationship that was undermined because of a lack of forgiveness? If so, explain.*

3. *Why do you think forgiveness is so important if you want to have friends that last a lifetime?*

Did you know that even the disciples wrestled with the issue of forgiveness? Though they walked with Jesus, they still struggled to wrap their minds around what it meant to forgive and how many times they were supposed to do it. Peter came to Jesus one day and asked specifically about the issue of forgiveness. The question he asks is a great one!

4. *Read **Matthew 18:21–22**. How many times does Jesus tell Peter that he should forgive? Do you think Peter was surprised by the response? Why or why not?*

Jesus goes on to illustrate His answer to Peter with a parable. He tells a story to illustrate just how important it is to forgive.

> 5. Read **Matthew 18:23–35**. What principle do you think Jesus is trying to illustrate in this parable?

> 6. Does focusing on how much God has forgiven you make you want to forgive others more or less? Explain.

Another parable in which Jesus illustrated the importance of forgiveness is the parable of the Prodigal Son. In this passage, we read of a forgiving father who embraced his son despite his poor choices.

> 7. Read **Luke 15:11–32**. How did the father respond to his son returning home? How is this response similar to the response of our heavenly Father?

8. *As you read this story, which character do you most identify with when it comes to the issue of forgiveness: the father, the son, or the older brother? Why?*

> *Forgiveness is not only one of the greatest gifts we can give someone, it's also one of the most powerful. Forgiveness has the ability to renew and restore friendships and allow them to become all God intended.*

Digging Deeper

Jesus never placed any limitations on forgiveness. In fact, He challenges all of us to forgive and continue forgiving. Read *Luke 6:27–36*. What portions of this passage come naturally to you? What portions of this passage are far more challenging? Why do you think Jesus challenges His followers to live in this way?

Ponder and Pray

The opening scripture for this lesson comes from *Matthew 6:14*: "For if you forgive men when they sin against you, your heavenly Father will also forgive you." Why do you think God's forgiveness of us and our forgiveness of others are linked? Is there anyone in your life that you need to forgive right now? Is there anyone in your life whom you need to ask forgiveness from?

Bonus Activity

Take out a sheet of paper and spend some time in prayer asking God to reveal anyone in your life with whom you may be harboring anger, resentment, or a hesitancy to forgive. As any names flash through your mind, write them down on the piece of paper. Spend some time asking God for the grace and strength to forgive each person. Then spend some time asking God to bless each person.

Eleven

The Power of Unity

*Make every effort to keep the unity of the Spirit
through the bond of peace.*

EPHESIANS 4:3

Jackie Robinson played second base for the Brooklyn Dodgers, but this wasn't what made him famous. Robinson was the first black man to play major league baseball. Throughout his career, in every game, he faced prejudiced people in the stands. Some booed him. Others taunted him. Still others ridiculed him.

One day, while playing a game in Brooklyn, Jackie made an error on the field. Immediately some of those in the stands began to heckle him. All eyes were on the ball player who was on second base. The words from the crowd were harsh and cruel. Unexpectedly, a fellow teammate and friend, Pee Wee Reese, walked on the field and stood bravely at Robinson's side. He placed his arm around the ball player and stood proudly beside him. Together, they faced the crowd. The fans grew silent. Later in his career, Jackie Robinson said that one moment with Reese standing beside him helped save his baseball career.

The power of friendship and the beauty of rich relationships cannot be measured. When we develop relationships with others, we develop strong bonds of unity, and we no longer have to face challenges on our own. Friendships can give us the strength to face any situation and stand in the face of adversity. Need proof? Just ask Jackie Robinson.

1. *Have you ever been through a situation where having a friend—and knowing that you weren't alone—made all the difference? Describe.*

2. *Why do think friendships are so important when it comes to facing difficult times? Do you think God designed us to experience rich, joyful friendships? Why or why not?*

One amazing story of friendship in the Bible is found between Elizabeth and Mary. Both became pregnant under some unusual circumstances, but as they spent time together, they found that God was doing something amazing in both of their lives and both of their families.

3. Read **Luke 1:39–56**. What kind of comfort and encouragement do you think Mary and Elizabeth found with each other during the three months they were together?

4. Who has been an Elizabeth or Mary to you in a particularly critical life stage?

Another wonderful display of unity in friendship is found in the story of Shadrach, Meshach, and Abednego, who chose to face the fiery furnace together.

5. Read **Daniel 3:1–30**. What comfort do you think Shadrach, Meshach, and Abednego had as they stood unified despite the king's decree (verses 17–18)? How do you think this story would have ended differently if they had not stood together in unity?

6. *Have you ever had anyone stand with you through a difficult ordeal? How did the experience change you? Your relationship? Your faith?*

7. *What are we encouraged to do in each of the following passages regarding our relationships and unity?*

   1 Corinthians 1:10:

   2 Corinthians 13:11:

   Philippians 1:27:

8. *Why do you think Scripture encourages us to live harmoniously and in unity? Why is that so important to our relationships with each other? What does it say to others who may be watching when you are living in peace and unity?*

Knowing that you are not alone is one of the most empowering truths! Not only is God with you, but He also places people beside you to celebrate the best and tackle the most difficult situations in life.

Digging Deeper

It's easy to get distracted by the differences we have with other people, but God calls us to live in unity—overlooking differences or even embracing them—to preserve love. Read *Galatians 3:28*. What does this verse mean to you right now in your own spiritual journey? Why do you think it's so important to see people as God sees them? How does looking at people through God's eyes empower you to love them even more?

Ponder and Pray

The opening scripture for this lesson comes from *Ephesians 4:3*: "Make every effort to keep the unity of the Spirit through the bond of peace." What efforts are you making right now to keep unity in your family? Your church? Your community?

Bonus Activity

Find a map of the world either online or in a book. Spend some time each day this week praying over different continents and nations of the world, asking God's peace to rule in those areas. Ask for unity among government officials to bring peace to particular regions.

Twelve

The Power of Celebration

*"My command is this: Love each other as I have
loved you. Greater love has no one than this, that
he lay down his life for his friends."*

JOHN 15:12–13

Remember the last time you saw two girls who were best friends
playing together? Odds are they were inseparable. Every little discovery became an opportunity to talk, share, and giggle. If you followed them for a few days, you'd see them eating together, playing
together, and probably even going to the bathroom together! They
may have even chosen to dress the same, share the same favorite
color, and develop silly rhyming nicknames for each other.

Though their parents probably weren't thrilled with the lack of
individuality, they appreciated the beauty of the friendship. Even as
little girls, we know how to celebrate our friends through talking,
sharing, and laughing. As we grow older, we need to hold onto these
celebration moments—times when we just appreciate being with
our friends because of who they are. Celebrating friends can be as

simple as enjoying lunch at a bistro on a lazy afternoon, sitting down on a comfy couch sipping a latte and talking about life, or finding a swing on a back porch and drinking a tall glass of sweet tea. Such moments remind us not just that we are loved but also that we have an amazing ability to love others and celebrate life with them.

As followers of Jesus, we have an incredible reason to celebrate others as we get glimpses into all that God is doing in our friends' lives. We can offer encouraging words, notes of affirmation, and even scriptures that celebrate God's love and goodness in life.

Let others know how you see God at work in their lives, and be a source of encouragement and celebration today!

You can begin celebrating your friends today! Invite someone to lunch. Ask someone to go on a walk. Choose to spend quality time together, and let them know how much you love and appreciate them. Let others know how you see God at work in their lives, and be a source of encouragement and celebration today!

1. *Have you ever celebrated someone just for being your friend? Have you ever been celebrated by someone else who is a friend? If so, describe.*

2. *What are some practical ways you can celebrate the friendships God has placed in your life?*

One of the greatest friendships that you have to celebrate is your relationship with God! God calls you not just His child but also His friend.

3. *Read **Romans 8:26–27**. In this passage, what does the Spirit do that shows just how close God really is to us?*

4. *How does it make you feel knowing that God understands when no one else understands?*

5. *What are some specific ways you can celebrate and nurture your relationship with God?*

Two people who developed a strong bond of friendship were Naomi and Ruth. Both went through an incredibly difficult time. Naomi lost her sons, and Ruth lost her husband. Naomi had already urged Ruth to return home, but Ruth was firm in deciding to stay because she chose to be loyal to Naomi.

6. Read **Ruth 1:16–17**. In what ways did Ruth's decision and words celebrate her friendship and affection for Naomi?

7. Have you ever had a friend who was a Ruth to you? Describe.

8. What are some ways in which you can celebrate the Ruths in your life?

As you grow new friends and keep the old, it's important to celebrate your friendships. Let the people you care about know that you care! Tell them. Serve them. Throw a celebration in their honor.

Digging Deeper

God designed us to live in relationships, encouraging and praying for each other. Read *James 5:13–20*. Have you ever had someone pray for you? How did it strengthen or help you? Have you ever confessed your sins to someone else? How did it strengthen your faith? Why do you think God designed us to live in relationships with others?

Ponder and Pray

The opening scripture for this lesson comes from *John 15:12–13*: "My command is this: Love each other as I have loved you. Greater love has no one than this, that he lay down his life for his friends." In what ways do you find this passage to be true? Have you ever had someone lay down his or her life for you? Have you ever laid down your life for someone else? Maybe it wasn't in the literal sense, but this could include any sort of sacrifice you made for someone else. What was the result? How did you grow through the experience?

Bonus Activity

Pick one friend and throw an appreciation party. It may be as simple as a surprise meal or outing. Consider inviting a few other friends to join in. Let the person know how much you appreciate them!

Leader's Guide

Chapter 1: One of Life's Greatest Gifts

Focus: *Friendships are a gift from God, meant to be celebrated and enjoyed. God is your Source for everything! We all need friends. Our friends help us grow into all God created us to be.*

1. *Answers will vary. This icebreaker question is designed to help participants recognize meaningful friendships in their lives and how friends can make life better.*

2. *Answers will vary. This question is designed to help participants recognize that friendship includes both giving and receiving, yet often when we give we receive back just as much or more in satisfaction and joy.*

3. *Answers will vary, but they may include activities like taking a walk, playing golf, quilting, tennis, sharing a meal, grabbing a cup of coffee, or going for a drive. The key is that friendships grow by spending time together, regardless of the activity.*

4. *Answers will vary, but the question is designed for participants to recognize the incredible importance of friendships for facing trials and adversity.*

5. *Answers*

Blessed are the . . .	What is their reward?
Poor in spirit	(example) The kingdom of God
Those who mourn	They will be comforted
The meek	They will inherit the earth
Those who hunger and thirst for righteousness	They will be filled
The merciful	They will be shown mercy
The pure in heart	They will see God
The peacemakers	They will be called sons of God
Those who are persecuted because of righteousness	Theirs is the kingdom of heaven
The insulted	Your reward is in heaven

6. *Answers will vary, but friends can teach us what it means to love, serve, or remain faithful in challenging times. Friends can remind us to find joy, peace, and hope. They can literally be little mirrors of God to us if we look closely.*

7. *Answers will vary, but in our friendships we have the opportunity to exhibit the fruits of the Spirit—to be patient, loving, and kind.*

8. *Answers will vary but include things like spending time together, offering encouraging words, delivering a small gift, or serving the person in a meaningful way.*

Chapter 2: Discovering God as a Best Friend

Focus: *God wants to be your best friend. He desires a relationship with you more than you can possibly imagine. He wants to be the first One you turn to in good times and bad.*

1. *Answers will vary, but the question is designed to help participants identify God's presence in their lives.*

2. *Answers will vary, but the question is designed to help participants identify moments when they've struggled to connect with God.*

3. *Answers will vary, but often when we look back on difficult situations, we discover that God was really there, and we can see His involvement in very specific ways.*

4. *Answers will vary, but this passage reveals the constancy of God. No matter what happens, He is true to His nature. He is a loving, kind God who keeps His covenants.*

5. *Answers will vary. It is a privilege and joy to be called a friend of God. We can feel like God is a close friend when we choose to spend time with Him through prayer, study His Word to get to know Him, and spend time in His presence. We may not feel like a friend of God when we neglect the relationship.*

6. *Answers will vary.*

7. *Nothing. The branches that don't remain in the vine are thrown into the fire and burned.*

8. *Answers will vary, but encourage participants who are willing to share their drawings.*

Chapter 3: Discovering God's Friends

Focus: *As a friend of God, you are called and created to love others. Loving others and loving God go hand in hand.*

1. *Answers will vary, but this question is designed to highlight the difference it makes in our lives when we are truly loved and accepted—just as we are. Love truly has a transformational impact.*

2. *Answers will vary, but this question is designed to help recognize the opportunities in our own lives to love others. Sometimes the simplest acts can have the biggest impact.*

3. *Answers will vary, but by keeping an open door in our hearts, we allow God's love to flow through us to others. We experience even more of God's love when we love others, and at times, those we love will become the ones who love us when we need it most.*

4. *Answers will vary. Some will find loving God easier, but others will find loving their neighbor easier. Both are meant to go hand in hand.*

5. *When we love others we reflect the love God has for us. We become extensions of Him and His love to the world around us.*

6. It's often easier to ignore the needs of others than to get involved in messy situations that will cost us. But the call as a follower of Christ is to get involved and become part of the solution.

7. Answers will vary. At times, all of us have been one of the three men described in the story.

8. Answers will vary, but this question is designed to compel participants to reflect on their own spiritual journeys and what God is calling them to do.

Chapter 4: Friends Who Teach Us Something

Focus: *Your life is enriched when you have friends you can learn from. Four friends to consider having: someone who can mentor you (like Paul), someone you can mentor (like Timothy), someone who shows love through quiet listening (like Mary), and someone who shows love through active service (like Martha).*

1. Answers will vary, but the question is designed to encourage participants to reflect on the richness of life that comes when we build relationships with a wide variety of people.

2. Paul describes Timothy as "my true son in the faith" and "my dear son." These tender terms reveal that Paul loved Timothy like a son. This description implies how close the two of them had grown over the years.

3. *Answers will vary, but mentoring someone and having someone who mentors you can enrich your life and be a powerful source of encouragement, strength, and growth.*

4. *Answers will vary, but your group may decide to start their own informal mentoring relationships by pairing women together who simply live life together by getting together once every few weeks for lunch or a walk. The key is being intentional about reaching out to someone else.*

5. *Mary responded to Jesus by sitting as His feet while Martha responded by serving Him. She allowed serving to distract her from what was truly important in the moment. Answers will vary regarding the sisters, but Mary was more relaxed and observant while Martha was more focused and hard-working.*

6. *Answers will vary. People like Mary teach us to seek God in the midst of the busyness and demands of the day.*

7. *Answers will vary. People like Martha remind us that part of loving God is serving Him and His people in very practical, tangible ways.*

8. *Answers will vary, but this question is designed to compel participants to take action and express gratitude to those who have made a difference in their life.*

Chapter 5: The Inner Circle of Friends

Focus: *When Jesus selected the disciples, He did not pick people who would become His followers, but those who would become His friends. His choices in the twelve disciples reveal something about the richness that comes from a diversity of friends as demonstrated in His relationships with John, Peter, Thomas, and Nathanael.*

1. *Answers will vary, but Jesus had hundreds of days with his disciples. They traveled together, ate together, fished together, and ministered together. In John 15:15, Jesus calls his disciples friends.*

2. *Answers will vary. The question is designed to help participants recognize just how different the disciples were in background and personalities. Undoubtedly, there were some definite sources of conflict among the group, but Jesus clearly loved every individual.*

3. *Answers will vary, but John identified himself as the "disciple whom Jesus loved." One of the reasons he did this was because in the process of becoming a follower and friend of Jesus, he found his identity in Christ. He was so aware of Jesus' love for him, it changed the way he described himself.*

4. *Answers will vary, but love manifests itself in word and deed.*

5. *Peter was the first to respond to Jesus' appearance. The story reveals that Peter was courageous and gutsy. He showed great*

faith in taking that first step with Jesus and demonstrated that he was willing to try new things and take risks.

6. *Thomas asks, "Lord, we don't know where you are going, so how can we know the way?" Jesus answers, "I am the way and the truth and the life. No one comes to the Father except through me. If you really knew me, you would know my Father as well. From now on, you do know him and have seen him." Those who ask tough questions challenge us to think, search for truth, and grow in our faith.*

7. *Jesus said of Nathanael, "Here is a true Israelite, in whom there is nothing false." Honest friends help keep us honest. They help us to remain true to who we are and who we were created to be.*

8. *Answers will vary.*

Chapter 6: Unexpected Friendships

Focus: *Some of the best and strongest friendships come from the most unexpected places and encounters. You may be surprised by some of the great friendships God gives you and the people who enrich your life. Four unexpected friends we find in the Bible are Lazarus, Joseph of Arimethea, Zacchaeus, and Onesimus.*

1. *Answers will vary, but all of us have grown from embracing people who are different from us. Often they teach us things about life and ourselves that we may not learn otherwise.*

2. *Answers will vary, but there can be struggles with communication, compassion, or understanding.*

3. *Answers will vary, but this story is a beautiful reminder that God's eyes are always on the poor. God invites us to serve and love Him by serving and loving others.*

4. *Answers will vary, but having a Lazarus in our lives allows us to share God's love and generosity in a tangible way. At the same time, we will discover lessons about ourselves and God we couldn't learn any other way.*

5. *Answers will vary, but you never really know the impact a gift can have on someone's life.*

6. *Answers will vary, but the scene to this story is set in such a way that Zacchaeus's response is surprising. Even Zacchaeus was probably surprised that Jesus would speak to him and ask to stay at his house.*

7. *Paul describes Onesimus in a variety of affectionate terms, including "my very heart," "a dear brother," "very dear to me," and "brother in the Lord." As followers of Jesus, we are invited to defend the defenseless and give voice to those who cannot speak on their own behalf. That's what Jesus did for us!*

8. *Answers will vary, but God wants us to keep our hearts open to others.*

Chapter 7: Untying Knots of Jealousy

Focus: *Jealousy can try to creep into any great friendship, but we can guard our relationships from jealousy by loving others and celebrating their successes.*

1. *Answers will vary, but this question is designed to help participants think about very specific things someone has done to encourage them.*

2. *Answers will vary, but there are countless ways we can get discouraged in everyday life. A kind word from a friend can make all the difference!*

3. *Answers will vary, but jealousy can creep into a relationship and undermine the love, care, and celebration of success that nurture a relationship.*

4. *He was jealous because Abel brought fat portions from some of his firstborn flock, and the Lord looked with favor on Abel and his offering but did not look with favor on Cain.*

5. *The Lord said to Cain: "Why are you angry? Why is your face downcast? If you do what is right, will you not be accepted? But if you do not do what is right, sin is crouching at your door; it desires to have you, but you must master it." Cain completely disregarded God's instruction and chose to attack and kill his brother.*

6. *Answers will vary.*

7. *Jonathan protected David from his father, Saul. He offered to do anything for David and set up a plan to let David know if Saul was truly against him.*

8. *Answers will vary.*

Chapter 8: Using Your Words as Balm

Focus: *Words are incredibly powerful! That's one reason it's so important to choose our words wisely and season our speech with love, grace, and kindness.*

1. *Answers will vary, but encouraging words literally lift our spirits. They make us want to reflect God's love and goodness to others.*

2. *Often discouraging words can do far more damage than we realize. Hurtful words that sting can cause all kinds of pain that lingers. That's why it's so important to choose our words wisely and graciously.*

3. *Answers will vary, but all of us have experienced the pain of being hurt by someone else's words or hurting someone else. The damage done can be immense.*

4. *Answers*

   Proverbs 11:9: *With his mouth the godless can destroy their neighbor.*

   Proverbs 13:3: *The one who guards his mouth preserves life but the one who opens wide comes to ruin.*

Proverbs 21:23: The one who guard his mouth guards his soul.

5. *Answers will vary.*

6. *Answers*

   Proverbs 16:24: Sweet words can bring healing to the bones.

   Isaiah 50:4: Wisely chosen words can sustain the weary.

   1 Peter 3:10: Those who want to love life and see good days should choose their words wisely.

7. *Answers will vary, but the key is being intentional about your conversations and times of worship with fellow followers of Jesus. Ideas may include getting together for times of worship, taking walks and praying together, or simply choosing to share what you're learning through Scripture over a latte.*

8. *Answers will vary.*

Chapter 9: Ensuring Selfishness Doesn't Win

Focus: *Friendships are so precious! We have to protect and guard them against selfishness, which can undermine a great relationship.*

1. *Answers will vary, but true friendship requires that we give to someone else and not just take. People who are selfish are often not fun to be around. Selfishness in a friendship can completely undermine the relationship by making one person want to pull away.*

2. *Answers will vary, but generally it comes down to being intentional about looking for opportunities to give, serve, and share. At the same time, it's important to be willing to ask for prayer and help in times of need. When a friend is there for you, always be quick to express and show gratitude.*

3. *The woman who had lost her son was selfish and wanted to take the second woman's son as her own. This woman was willing to go as far as to have the child killed to make sure the other woman didn't get to keep her child.*

4. *He knew that the true mother would not be as selfish as to allow her son to die.*

5. *Some of the fruit includes disorder and every evil practice. Selfishness can kill a friendship.*

6. *We are to walk with the wisdom of God. We are to look to that which is pure, peace-loving, considerate, submissive, impartial, sincere, and full of mercy and good fruit. Those who are peacemakers will reap a rich harvest.*

7. *Answers will vary, but Philippians encourages us to do nothing out of selfish ambition or vain conceit. We are to walk in humility, considering others better than ourselves. We are not only to serve our own interests but also the interests of others.*

8. *When we keep our eyes on Jesus and what's truly important eternally, then we realize that it's not all about us, but all about serving and loving others. Jesus calls us to lay down our lives for others and give generously to those we know and those in need.*

Chapter 10: The Power of Forgiveness

Focus: *Forgiveness is not only one of the greatest gifts we can give someone, it's also one of the most powerful. Forgiveness has the ability to renew and restore friendships and allow them to become all God intended.*

1. *Answers will vary, but this question is designed to get participants to discuss the beauty and wonder of forgiveness.*

2. *Answers will vary, but it's amazing to see how grudges cut us off from being all God created us to be.*

3. *In every friendship, there will be moments of disagreement, miscommunication, and unintentional hurt. If these issues are not brought up and dealt with through forgiveness, then one or both people in a relationship may harbor resentment, anger, or bitterness that can completely destroy a relationship. That's one reason it's important to forgive—and to do it fast!*

4. *Jesus tells Peter he is supposed to forgive seventy-seven times! In other words, we are to forgive and keep on forgiving. Forgiveness has no limit or end. Now that doesn't mean that you need to keep submitting yourself to a hurtful or harmful situation. But when grievances arise, the best possible thing you can do is forgive. Peter was probably shocked by the generosity of Jesus' answer. To forgive seven times was a lot, but seventy-seven must have seemed unimaginable.*

5. *Answers will vary, but Jesus is illustrating that when it comes to forgiveness, we need to realize just how much we've been forgiven of. In our own lives, it's all too easy to hold something against someone else until we realize that God has forgiven us for even more. We have been shown mercy, and we are to extend that mercy to others.*

6. *Focusing on how much God has forgiven us should make us want to be all the more forgiving, because none of us are worthy of God's forgiveness.*

7. *The father responded by running to his son, throwing his arms around him, and kissing him. The son asked for forgiveness, and the father quickly accepted his apology. He gave his son his best robe, a ring (signifying that he was again a member of the family), and sandals. He threw a celebration.*

8. *Answers will vary, but depending on age or stage in life, participants may identify with the father, especially if they've been struggling with their own prodigal child. They may identify with the son if they've been living apart from God or choosing unhealthy activities. Or they may identify with the older brother if they see others experiencing good things despite their bad actions. All of us at one time or another will identify with each of the characters in the parable of the Prodigal Son. But the lesson remains the same: all of us are invited to choose forgiveness.*

Chapter 11: The Power of Unity

Focus: *Knowing that you are not alone is one of the most empowering truths! Not only is God with you, but He also places people beside of you to celebrate the best and tackle the most difficult situations in life.*

1. *Answers will vary, but this question is designed to remind participants that at times our friends are what make the difference in getting through a tough situation. There is an immense strength in knowing that we're not alone and that God sends people to walk along side of us.*

2. *We all need people to talk to, those who can listen, as well as those who can offer words of encouragement and prayer. God designed us to be in relationship with each other.*

3. *Answers will vary, but undoubtedly they talked about their pregnancies, the amazing things that were happening to their bodies, and the unusual experiences surrounding their babies' conceptions. This is a wonderful story of God bringing women together to encourage each other during a challenging time.*

4. *Answers will vary.*

5. *Answers will vary, but undoubtedly, the three men stood stronger because they were together. Answers of how things may have ended differently are mere speculation and open to guesses, but because they did stand together, they were all rewarded together!*

6. *Answers will vary.*

7. *Answers*

    1 Corinthians 1:10: *"I appeal to you, brothers, in the name of our Lord Jesus Christ, that all of you agree with one another so that there may be no divisions among you and that you may be perfectly united in mind and thought."*

    2 Corinthians 13:11: *"Finally, brothers, good-by. Aim for perfection, listen to my appeal, be of one mind, live in peace. And the God of love and peace will be with you."*

    Philippians 1:27: *"Whatever happens, conduct yourselves in a manner worthy of the gospel of Christ. Then, whether I come and see you or only hear about you in my absence, I will know that you stand firm in one spirit, contending as one man for the faith of the gospel."*

8. *Answers will vary, but God designed people before the Fall to live in peace with Him and each other. When we embrace unity, our friendships grow deeper and we naturally become a testimony of God's goodness and grace to those around us.*

Chapter 12: The Power of Celebration

Focus: *As you grow new friends and keep the old, it's important to celebrate your friendships. Let the people you care about know that you care! Tell them. Serve them. Throw a celebration in their honor.*

1. *Answers may vary, but celebrating a friend can be as simple as offering encouraging words, sending a card, or throwing a party. Celebration takes many forms but always displays gratitude and appreciation.*

2. *Everything from handwritten cards to gifts to quality time can be forms of celebration.*

3. *He searches our hearts and knows our deepest thoughts. He even understands our groans and prays for us.*

4. *Answers will vary, but it's of great comfort that God is so close to us!*

5. *Words of praise and worship can express gratitude and thankfulness to God for who He is and all He has done. Spending time in prayer to both speak and listen can help nurture a relationship with God. And, of course, spending time reading Scripture can illuminate attributes of God you may never have seen before.*

6. *Ruth's faithful friendship and loyalty to Naomi provided comfort and companionship for both women during a challenging time.*

7. *Answers will vary.*

8. *Answers will vary.*

About the Author

Margaret Feinberg is an author and speaker who offers a refreshing perspective on faith and the Bible. She has written more than a dozen books including *The Organic God* and *God Whispers*. She also wrote The Women of Faith Bible Study *Overcoming Fear*. Margaret is a popular speaker at women's events, luncheons, and retreats as well as national conferences including Catalyst, LeadNow, Fusion, and the National Pastor's Conference.

She lives in Lakewood, Colorado, in the shadow of the Rockies with her 6'8" husband, Leif. When she's not writing and traveling, she loves hiking, shopping, blogging, laughing, and drinking skinny vanilla lattes with her girlfriends. But some of her best days are spent communicating with her readers.

So if you want to put a smile on her face, go ahead and write her!

Margaret@margaretfeinberg.com

www.margaretfeinberg.com

www.margaretfeinberg.blogspot.com

Tag her on Facebook or follow her on twitter

www.twitter.com/mafeinberg

Additional Resources

What Shall We Study Next?

Women of Faith® has numerous study guides out right now
that will draw you closer to God.

Visit www.womenoffaith.com or www.thomasnelson.com
for more information.

Being Yourself
How Do I Take Off This Mask?

*Jesus said to him, "If I will that he remain
till I come, what is that to you? You follow Me."*

JOHN 21:22, NKJV

Who are you? It's one of the simplest but most difficult questions for anyone to answer. Most people spend their lifetime trying to figure out who they really are. Some of their efforts are healthy and rewarding, but others can be dangerous and even destructive. As a follower of Jesus, you don't have to spend years wondering who you really are! You get to go straight to the source—God—to discover not only who you are but who you are created to be.

If you wanted to truly understand a painting, who would you ask? The person who purchased the painting? The person who framed the painting? The museum curator? While all those individuals may have insight, the best possible person to ask would be the artist. In the same way, God invites you to understand yourself in the light of who He has created you to be.

Why is it so important to go to God to discover who you really are? Because He's the only one who really knows. He created you. He knows you like no other. You have gifts and talents and desires tucked inside of you that you may not even know about, but God does!

In this study, you're going to discover who you really are in God's eyes. You're going to learn how simply being yourself sets others free to be themselves. You will have the opportunity to evaluate the unique strengths, gifts, and talents God has given you and how to better use them to serve and love others. And you're going to recognize the rich fruit that grows naturally in your life when you're simply being yourself.

My hope and prayer for you is that through this study you will begin to see yourself as God sees you—beautiful, redeemed, and wonderfully made.

Blessings,

Margaret Feinberg

Resting in Him
I Need to Slow Down, But I Can't!

*The LORD replied, "My Presence will go with you,
and I will give you rest."*

EXODUS 33:14

Rest. Our souls crave it. Our bodies demand it. Our spirits are renewed through it. Yet rest is one of those treasures that we often don't take the time to enjoy in the busyness of life. As the pace of our modern world speeds up, we find ourselves trying to do more in the same amount of time. Left unchecked, we become experts in efficiency—running hard and fast on the treadmill of life. Our souls grow weary. Our bodies grow weak. Our spirits run dry.

When asked what a person truly needs to survive, most people list air, water, and food, while forgetting that rest is also vitally important to our bodies, minds, and spirits. Rest has the power to transform our attitudes, our actions, and even our activities. When well-rested, we are better equipped to face the challenges as well as the occasional curveball daily life often throws at us.

Meanwhile, the God who formed and shaped us offers us rest— *real rest*—in Him. He invites us to step off the treadmill of life and discover the renewal and restoration that can only come from Him. When we take time to rest, we begin to realize that what feels like doing nothing is really allowing God to do something inside of us. Our souls are given a chance to renew. Our physical bodies are given a chance to heal. Our spirits are given the opportunity to connect with God. In those precious moments, we are reminded not just of who we are but whose we are. Afterward, we find ourselves echoing a common response, *I needed that!*

The ultimate rest you will ever experience doesn't just take place during a nap or a lazy Sunday afternoon. Instead, it's found in God. He is the One who renews your weary soul. He is the One who gives you strength when you think you can't go any farther—emotionally, physically, spiritually, and relationally. The rest that God provides is like no other. Don't you think it's time that you take a break and enter into the rest God has for you?

My hope and prayer is that through this study, you will discover real rest—the kind that God has specifically designed for you—and learn to relax in the arms of your Savior.

Blessings,

Margaret Feinberg

WOMEN OF FAITH
DEVOTIONAL JOURNAL

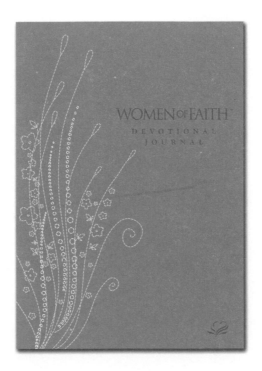

*T*he *Women of Faith Devotional Journal*
speaks directly to the subject of God's infinite grace. Filled with
stirring quotes and uplifting Scripture, this journal is the ideal
addition to any devotional time.

- SCRIPTURE VERSES HIGHLIGHT WISDOM FOR DAILY LIFE

- YOUR FAVORITE WOMEN OF FAITH SPEAKERS' ENLIGHTENING
  THOUGHTS ON GRACE

- PLENTY OF WRITING SPACE TO RECORD DREAMS, HOPES,
  AND PERSONAL REFLECTIONS

WOMEN OF FAITH

THOMAS NELSON
Since 1798